FRANCIS POULENC

SONATA
For Clarinet and Bassoon

> **WARNING:** the photocopying of any pages of this publication is illegal. If copies are made in breach of copyright, the Publishers will, where possible, sue for damages.
>
> Every illegal copy means a lost sale. Lost sales lead to shorter print runs and rising prices. Soon the music goes out of print, and more fine works are lost from the repertoire.

CHESTER MUSIC

à Madame Audrey PARR

SONATA
For Clarinet and Bassoon

Francis POULENC
(1922)
Revised by the composer
March, 1945

I. Allegro

ff en dehors
f
p
mf
f
2
mf
f
mf
en dehors
pp
ff très sec
stacc.
mf
p
3
f
p

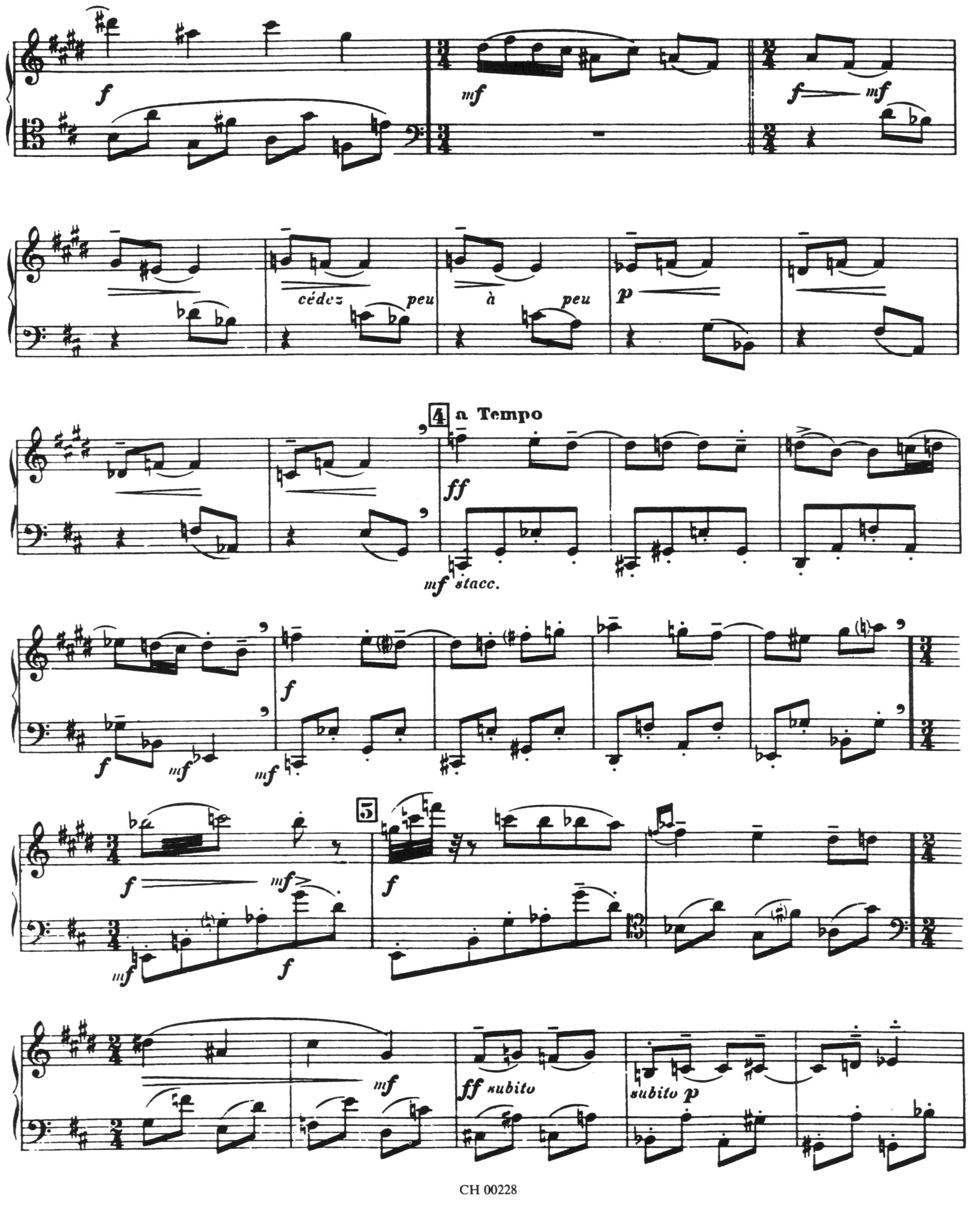
cédez peu à peu
4 a Tempo
mf stacc.
5
ff subito
subito p

6
cédez
ff
mf stacc.
mf
ff
8
ff strident
stacc.
ff
ff
f
très marqué
mf
ff
mp
mf
f staccato
mf
staccatissimo
p

II. Romance

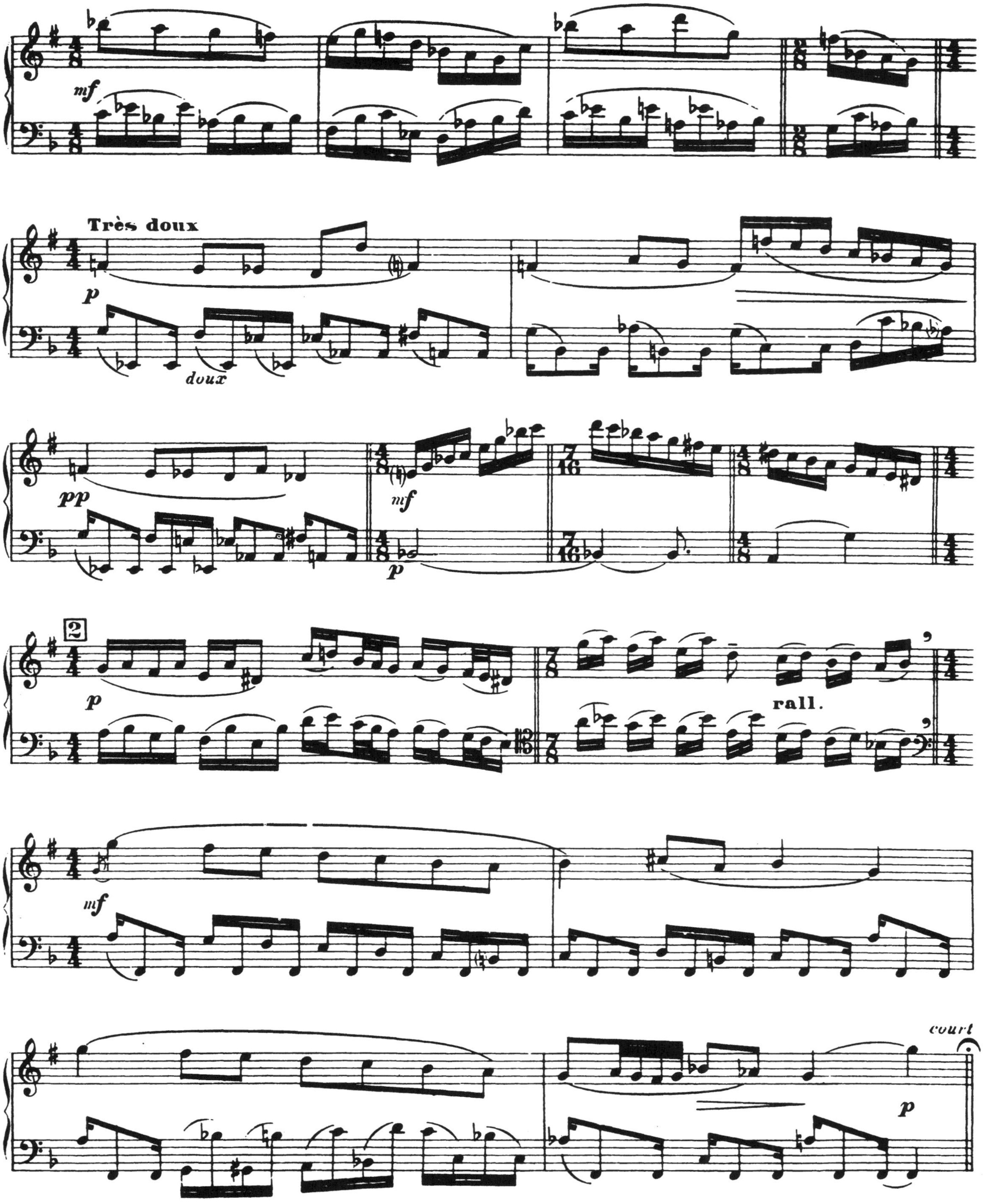
mf
Très doux
p
doux
pp
mf
p
2
p
rall.
mf
court
p

III. Final

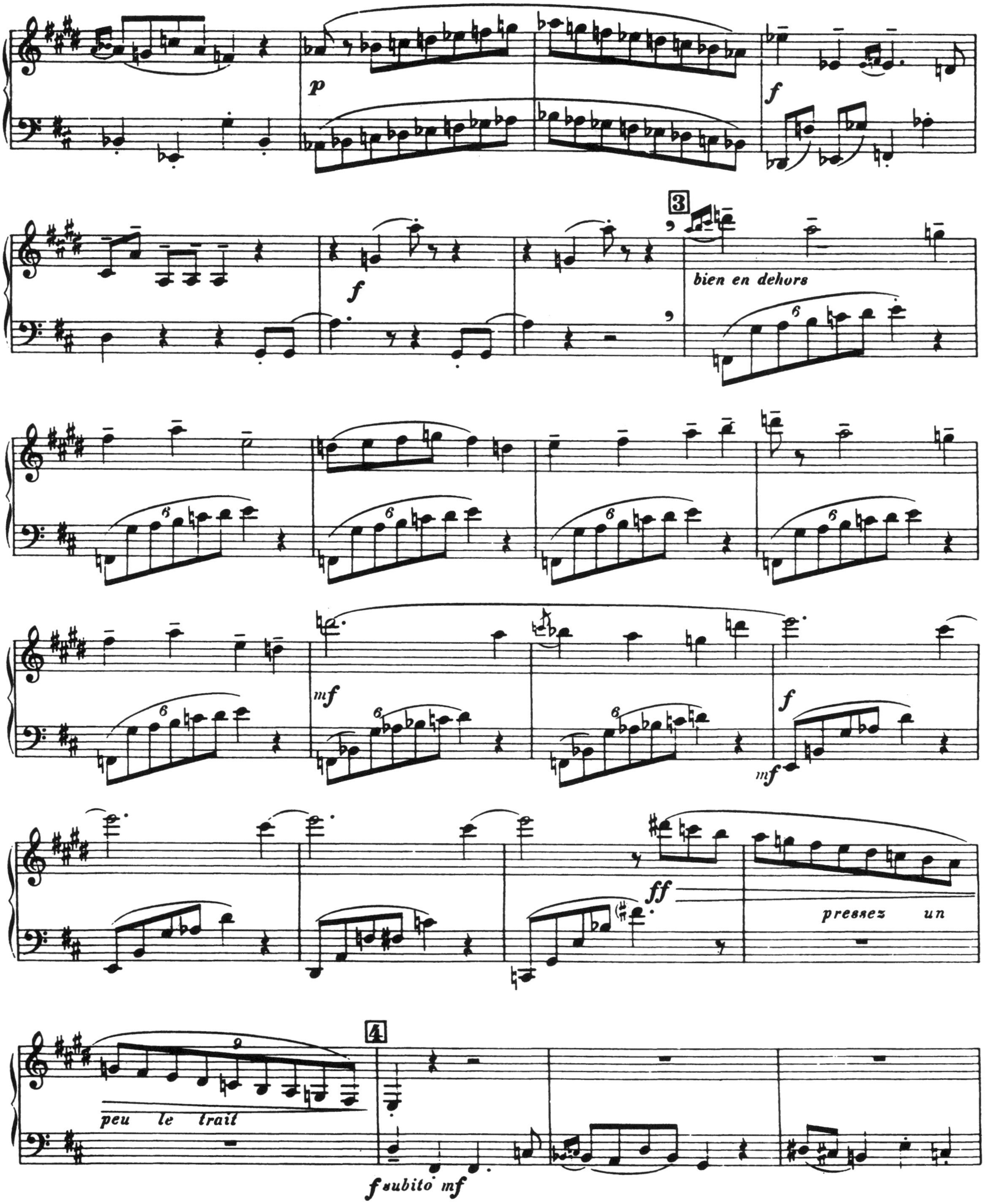
3
bien en dehors
pressez un
peu le trait
4
f subito mf

f
mf
f
ra - len - tir peu à peu
ralentir encore
mf
silence
5
Andante - Mouv^t romance (♪ = 72)
cantando
mf en accompagnant
mf dolce

pp
6
Subito tempo vite (𝅗𝅥 = 120)
p
f
ff
mf
f
7
mf
cédez
mf
8
Presto (𝅗𝅥 = 130)
très accentué

Printed and bound in Great Britain by Caligraving Limited

Touraine - Septembre - 1922